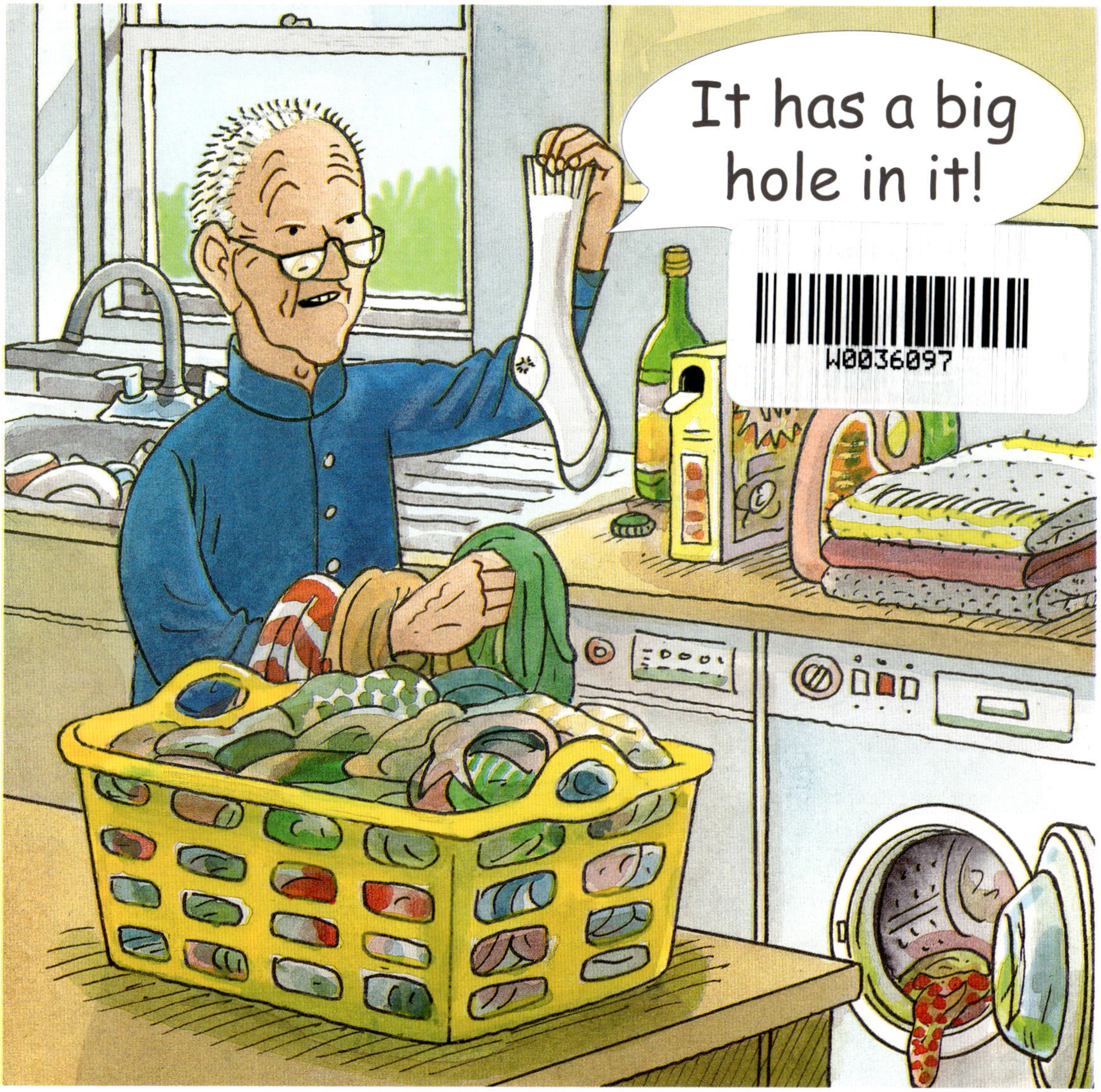


Grandpa Chen had a sock.

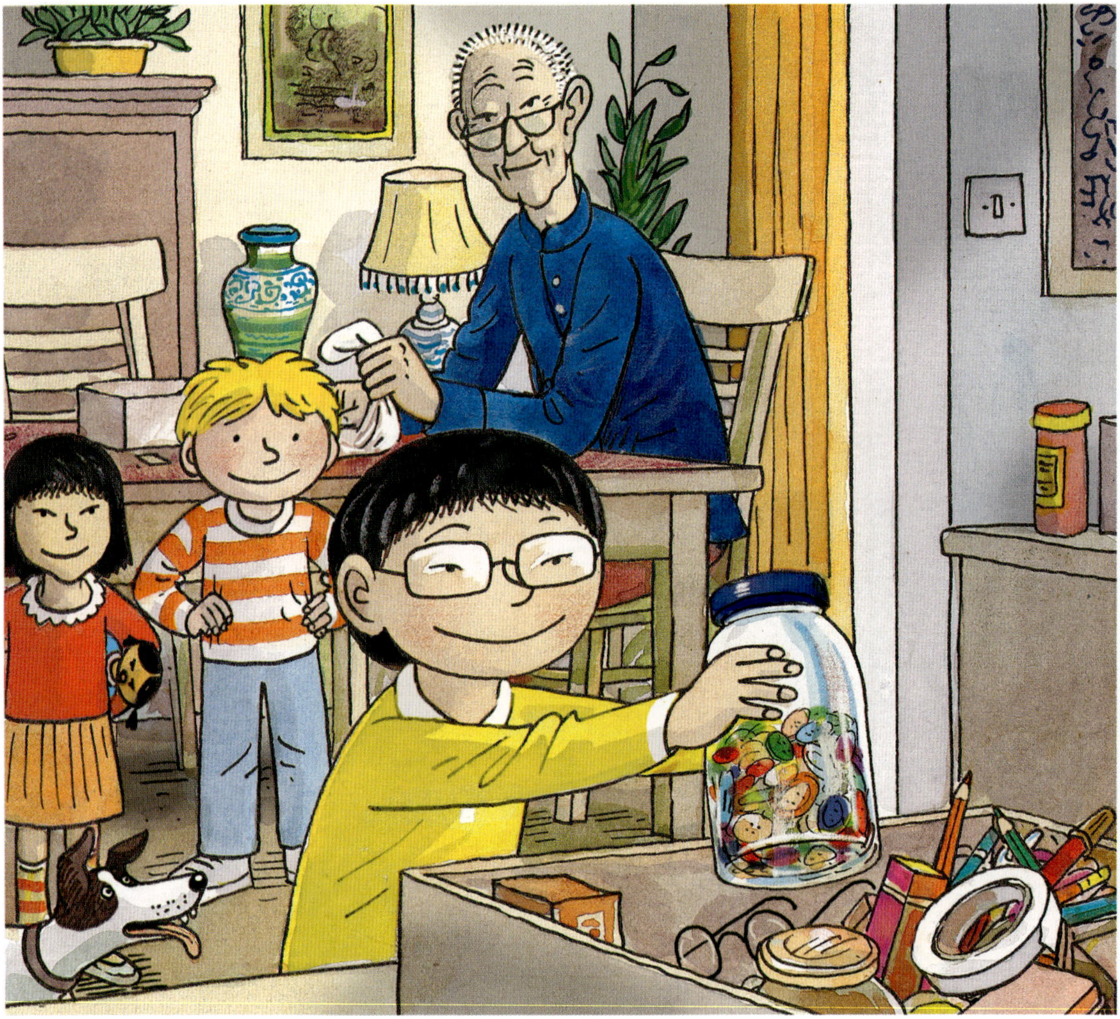

Lee went to get buttons.

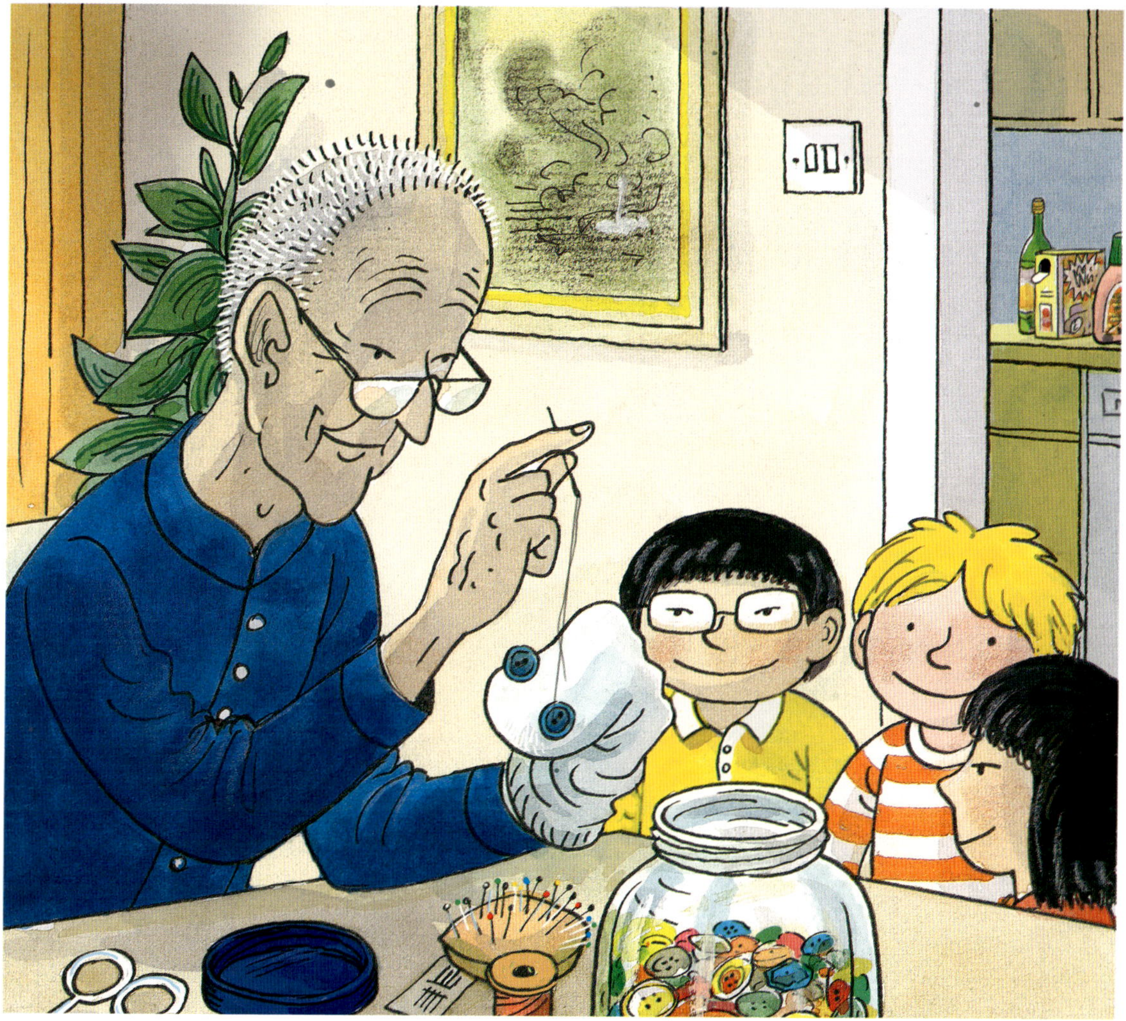

Grandpa Chen put the buttons on the sock.

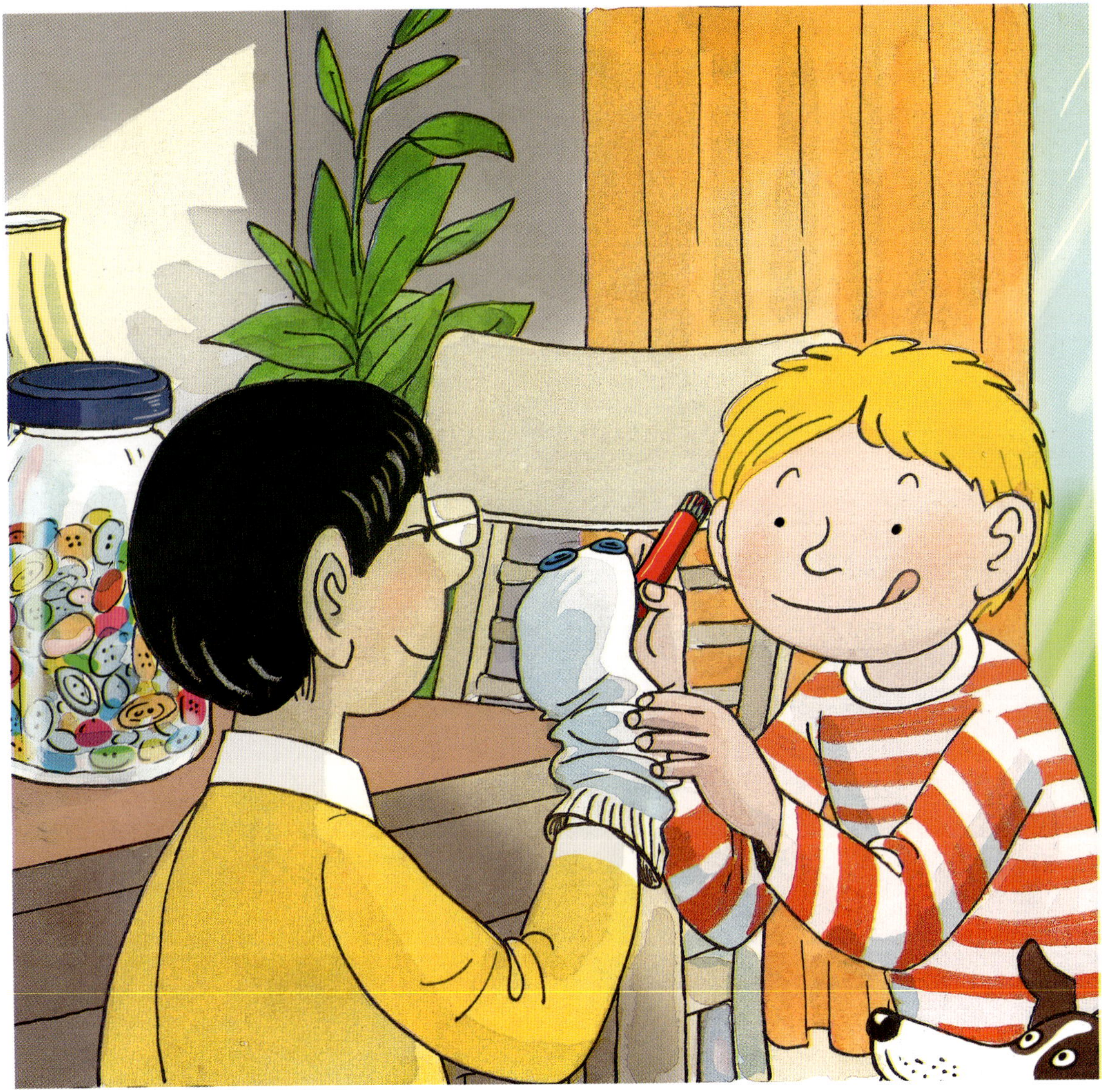

Kipper got a red pen.

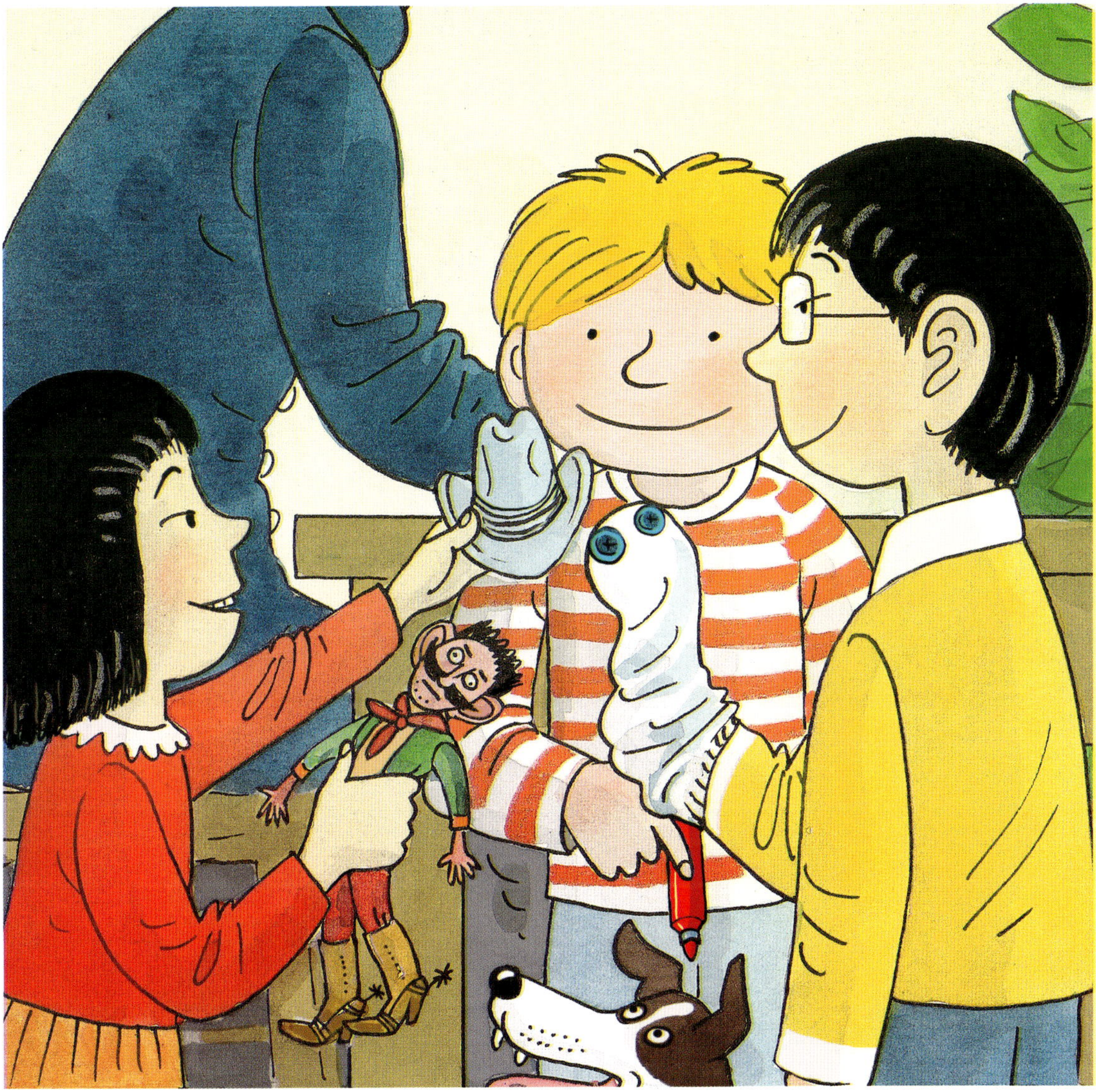

Lin got a cowboy hat.

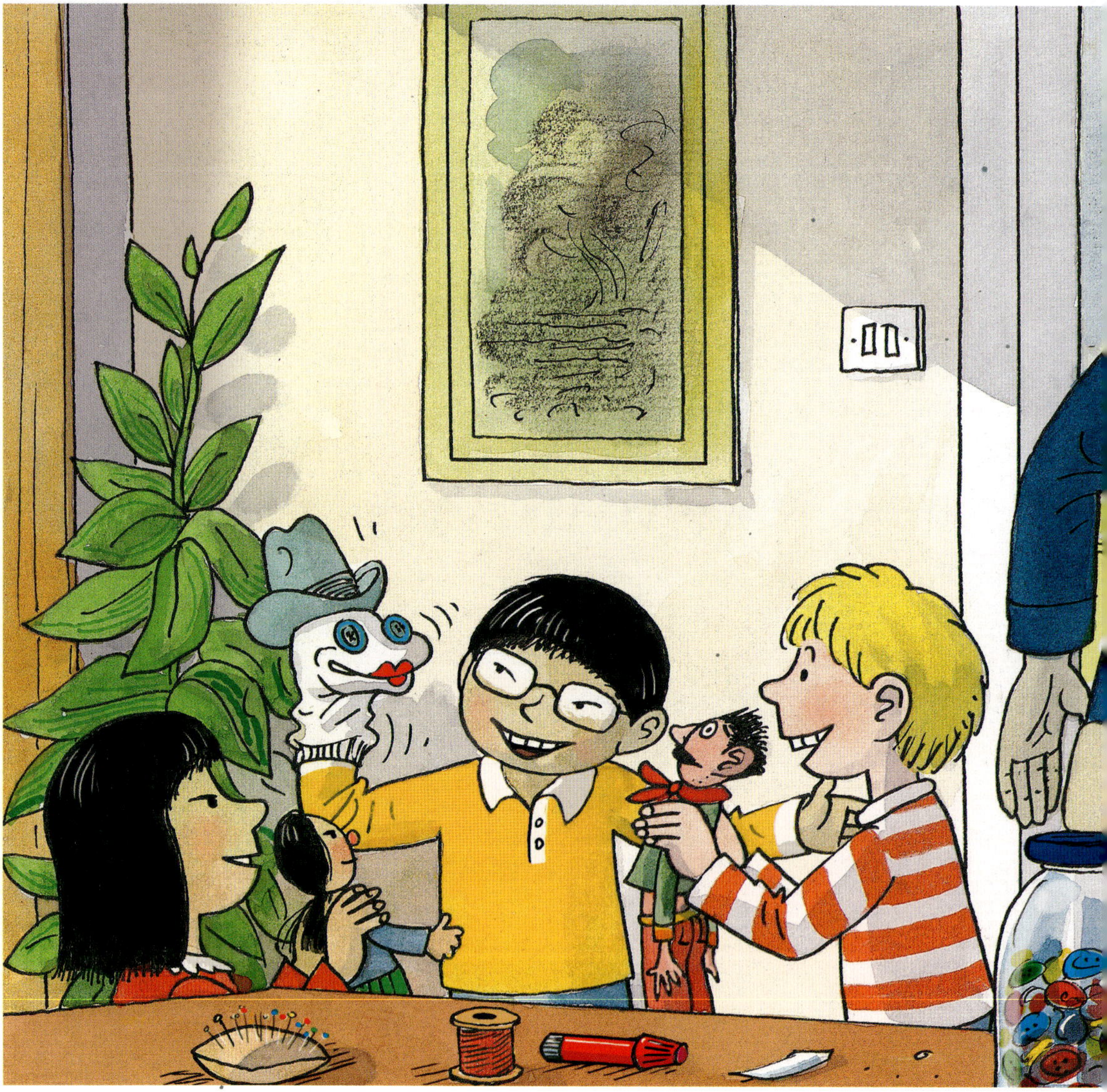

The sock was a lot of fun.

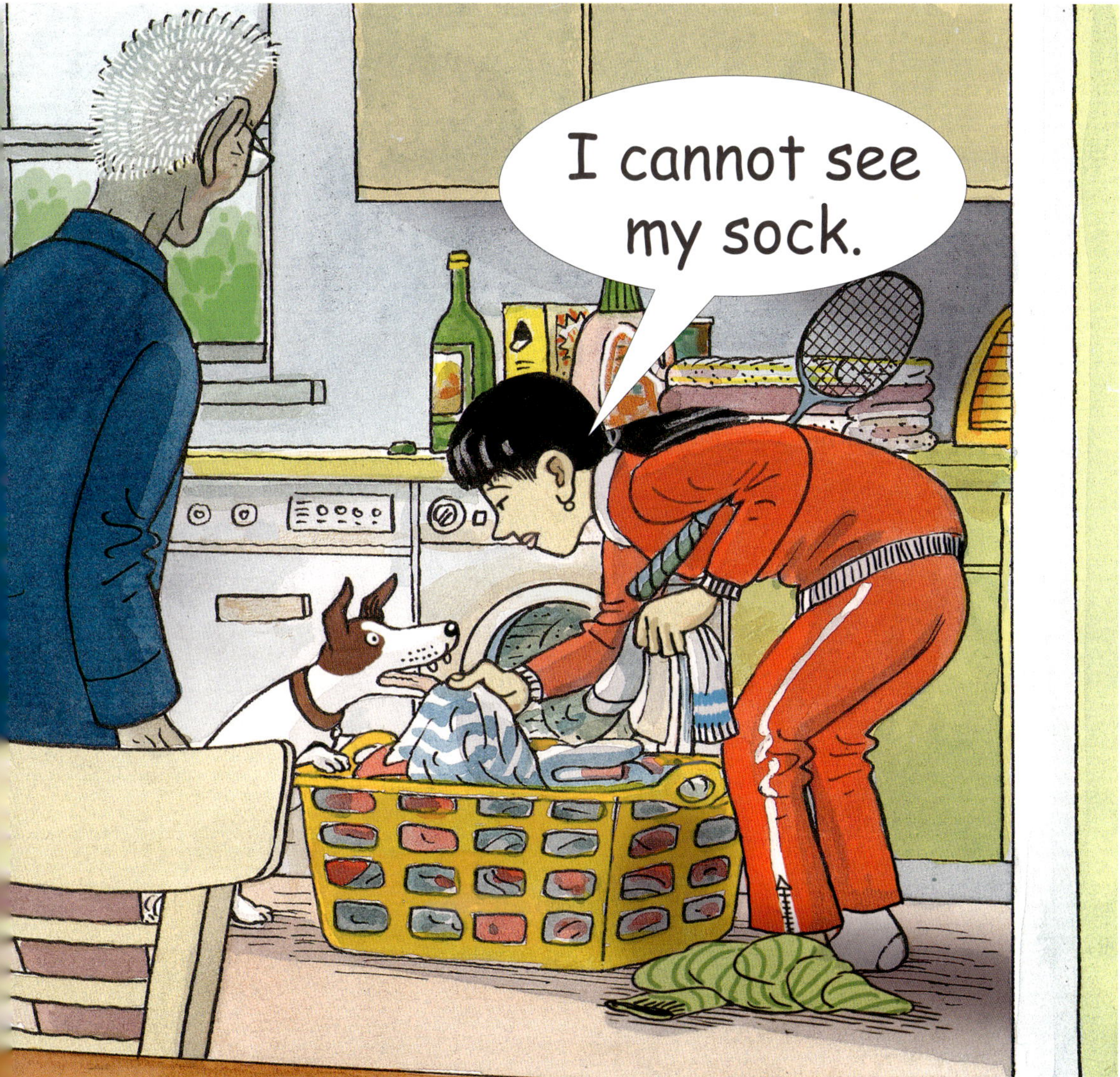
I cannot see my sock.

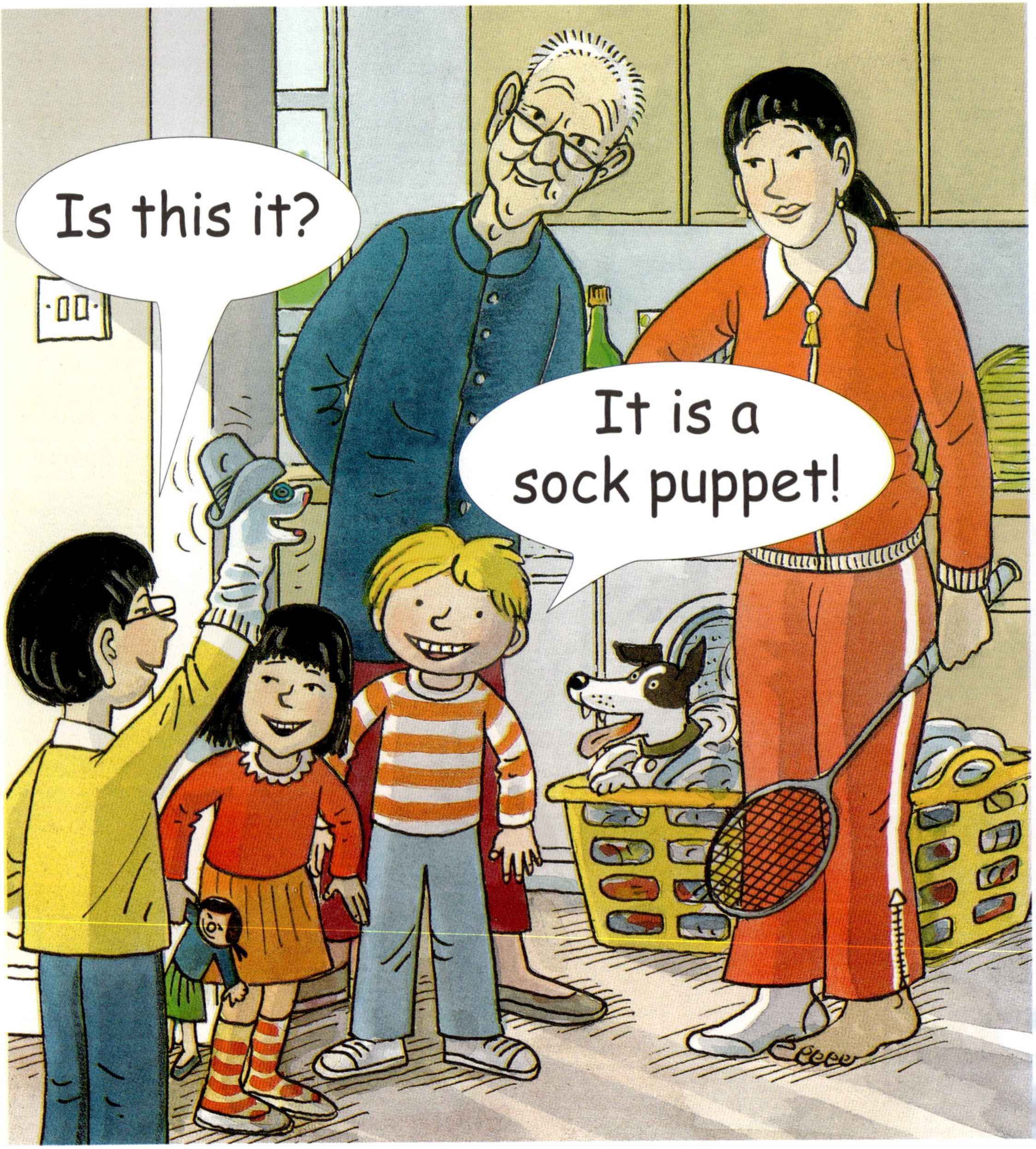
Is this it?
It is a sock puppet!